The Clapham Sect

Margaret Bryant

THE CLAPHAM SOCIETY

2004

Acknowledgements

The Clapham Society is grateful for the co-operation of the copyright holders for permission to reproduce the following illustrations. Whilst every effort has been made to trace copyright holders we regret that this has not always been possible.
Anti-Slavery International (covers and 42, 63)
Guildhall Library, Corporation of London (8)
Holy Trinty Church, Clapham (4, 11, 13, 49, 51)
National Portrait Gallery, London (8, 16, 38, 46)
South London Press (38)
US Library of Congress (19)
Victoria and Albert Museum, London (16)

The Clapham Society would like to record its appreciation of the work of the late Ann King-Hall, who typed the first draft, and would like to thank the following members of the Society's Local History Sub-Committee for their painstaking scrutiny of the text: Annabel Allott, Eleanor Grey, Bernard Middleton, David Perkin and Alyson Wilson

Edited by Peter Jefferson Smith

Designed by Derrick McRobert MCSD MSTD

Published by The Clapham Society, 22 Crescent Grove, London SW4 7AH

Printed by Cantate, telephone 020 7622 3401 www.canate.biz

© The Clapham Society and Margaret Bryant 2004

ISBN : 0 9500694 6 9

Front cover: Monument to Charles James Fox (died 1807) in Westminster Abbey, with kneeling slave.
Front and back covers: Medallions commemorating the abolition of negro apprenticeship in the West Indies, 1838.

The Clapham Sect

TABLE OF CONTENTS

Page		
	5	Foreword
	7	**An age of revolution**
	9	**A fraternity bound by religion**
	14	**The fight against slavery begins** – Granville Sharp – Thomas Clarkson – William Wilberforce
	23	**The friends come to Clapham** –The Thornton family – John Venn – Henry Thornton – Charles Grant – John Shore, Lord Teignmouth – James Stephen – Zachary Macaulay – Granville Sharp in old age – William Smith
	35	**Christian mission** – Australia – India – The Church Missionary Society – Mission at home – The Bible Society
	43	**Abolition of the slave trade** – Wilberforce's critics
	50	**Abolition of slavery**
	52	**The heritage of the Clapham Sect** – Shaping world history – Imperialism and mission
	57	**Epilogue**
	59	References
	60	Biographical notes
	62	Reading
	64	Index

"Am I not a man and a brother?"
Ceramic medallion promoting abolition, made by Wedgwood,
now in possession of Holy Trinity Church, Clapham Common.

Foreword

Ours is a divided world. Internationally, the UK is part of a prosperous group of nations, enjoying greater wealth, even as global inequalities increase. Ours is a consumer society, where individualism reigns. Other parts of the world see dire poverty, disease, exploitation and war. World instability is growing.

Even at home, we are not at ease. Our society is divided between haves and have-nots; we are anxious about crime; we are cynical about politicians and sleaze. Religion may be seen as a pastime of a minority or (in its extreme forms) a threat to our stability.

We have been here before. There are many parallels in history between today and the late 1780s to 1810. The industrial revolution and the explosion of European world trade had created a new capitalism and wealth for a fortunate few. The other side of the coin was crime, revolution in the United States and France, slavery and injustice for the poor.

A group of rich, influential British men and women set out to challenge the moral climate of their times and, in doing so, changed the world.

The Clapham Sect was a group of busy professionals living in Clapham around the Common, many of whom had made fortunes through trade. They were mainly evangelical Anglicans who made time for Christian deeds and who gave liberally to worthy causes. Their efforts ranged across a broad spectrum of issues: their main achievement was abolition of the slave trade in 1807; abolition of the institution of slavery itself followed in 1833. Their work also encompassed Christian missions, education, public morality and provision for the poor.

After their success in persuading Parliament to outlaw the slave trade, William Wilberforce said to his friend Henry Thornton: "Well

Henry, what shall we abolish next?" That might be a question to us.

The Clapham Society welcomes Margaret Bryant's account of the Clapham Sect. It should be both a challenge and an inspiration for us to set an example; taking leadership to work towards a neighbourly society based, not on individualism, but on community and moral integrity, responsible not just to our neighbours at home, but to the wider world.

PETER JEFFERSON SMITH
The Clapham Society   March 2004

MARGARET BRYANT

MARGARET BRYANT is a retired teacher of history. A graduate of Cambridge University, she was Reader in Education at the University of London Institute of Education. She has written extensively in the area of education, with emphasis on secondary education in London and the pioneering of women's education in the nineteenth century. She has contributed a number of biographies of women educationalists to the *Oxford Dictionary of National Biography*, to be published in 2004. A resident of Clapham, she has been for many years a member of Holy Trinity Church and of the Clapham Society.

An age of revolution

THE LAST DECADES OF THE EIGHTEENTH CENTURY and the early decades of the nineteenth century have been called the Age of Elegance by one historian Arthur Bryant, and by Percy Bysshe Shelley, who lived through them, the Age of Despair. They were Clapham's finest hour. For the first time what was happening in Clapham can be seen to be a pivot of world history.

In Britain this was the period when a modern society and economy were painfully struggling into being amidst turmoil, violence, dislocation, bewilderment. The hand-loom and the spinning wheel were being replaced by power-driven machinery. The packhorse and the saddle gave way to the stage coach, the canal and eventually the railway. Early industrialisation was accompanied by an emerging population explosion. Britain, having lost its first empire in the American Revolution or War of Independence (1776–83), was beginning to build an ever wider world dominion. Political, legal, penal and social institutions were quite unprepared to cope with such changes.

All this was happening at a time of prolonged and desperate war (1794–1815) against revolutionary and then Napoleonic France, when our hereditary rulers, thrown into panic by fear of revolution at home, resorted to repression of ferocious and unjustifiable dimensions.

Such challenges needed a moral response, a response of the will, and this was found in Clapham. Then a prosperous and healthy village, it was in easy riding or driving distance of the City of London and Westminster, and was provided with one of the earliest regular horse omnibus services. It became the home and headquarters of a remarkable group, which gained from fashionable and frivolous or unsympathetic observers the derisive names of "The Clapham Sect" or "Patent Christians" or simply "The Saints".

They, as true prophets should, discerned the times. Their beliefs, their perseverance, their gruelling hard work, their abilities created a moral climate which permanently changed national and even international convictions and policies. Their methods provided the new age with practices and organisations which made their work effective and rallied public opinion and support from the all-important new middle classes. Their greatest crusade was for the abolition of the slave trade and then of slavery itself.

The Cock Pond and
Holy Trinity Church, Clapham, circa 1820.
inset: Henry Venn.

A fraternity bound by religion

CONSIDERING THEIR IMPACT ON HISTORY the list of the fraternity seems surprisingly short. There was in fact no 'membership' and the memorial plaque on the south wall of Holy Trinity Church on Clapham Common includes only some of those who worshipped there – Granville Sharp (1735–1813), Charles Grant MP (1746–1823), John Shore (Lord Teignmouth) (1751–1834), William Smith MP (1756–1835), John Venn (1759–1833), James Stephen MP (1758–1832), William Wilberforce MP (1759–1833), Henry Thornton MP (1760–1815), Zachary Macaulay (1768–1838).

There were others in Clapham who worked closely with them, for example, Edward Eliot MP (1759–97), brother-in-law of the Prime Minister William Pitt, a valuable link in the political network before his early death. Charles Elliott (1751–1832) was a prosperous silk merchant with a Bond Street upholstery business patronised by royalty. He was John Venn's brother-in-law, actively concerned with nearly all the Sect's causes and crusades – a valiant associate. Thomas Clarkson (1760–1846) never lived in Clapham, but close and invaluable association must give him honorary membership.

There were also 'country members' who worked closely and stayed often with Clapham friends. Thomas Babington MP (1758–1837) was squire of Rothley Temple in Leicestershire and Member of Parliament for the county, a tireless abolitionist and married to a Macaulay. He was responsible for introducing Zachary Macaulay to the group.

Thomas Gisborne (1758–1846), the perpetual curate of Yoxall in Staffordshire, had known William Wilberforce since their days at Cambridge and became so much involved with the Sect that his parish was known as a Second Clapham.

Mrs Hannah More (1745–1833) was one of five sisters who kept a successful girls' school in Bristol. Hannah More was well educated, charming, witty and warm-hearted and made a name for herself as a dramatist and writer. She was welcomed in London literary and fashionable society, where she became something of a fashion herself, praised by Dr Johnson, and a friend of Sir Joshua Reynolds, David Garrick and Horace Walpole, and taken up by the Blue Stocking coteries of learned ladies. She also met philanthropists engaged in the early abolition cause and it was by this route that she was swept into the orbit of the Sect, a valuable recruit, keen and competent, one of the "best men of the cause". When she met William Wilberforce, a warm friendship quickly grew between the young man and the middle-aged lady, and their collaboration appears frequently in the saga of the Sect.

This unique Clapham fraternity was, in fact, no sect, but that name has a certain appropriateness and has clung to them ever since it was coined, perhaps by the Reverend Sydney Smith. The majority were loyal Anglicans. They were bound together by what they called Vital Religion, their conviction that they were under divine guidance and discipline. Their evangelical zeal was little favoured, however, by the Anglican establishment which still tended to believe that enthusiasm was, as Bishop Butler said to John Wesley, "a horrid thing, a very horrid thing".

Throughout the country there were pockets of this vital Christianity, for example in Huddersfield, where Henry Venn (1725–97) who had been curate of Clapham, had his incumbency, and from where he drew much of the industrial North into the fold. Above all Cambridge: here Charles Simeon (1759–1836) Vicar of Holy Trinity and a fellow of King's, and Isaac Milner (1750–1820) Dean of Carlisle and President of Queens', had a powerful influence. In the City of London there were few evangelical clergy but at St Mary Woolnoth in Lombard Street, John Newton (1725–1807) former slave trader and friend of the poet William Cowper (together they produced the Olney Hymns) was incumbent.[1]

These Anglican evangelicals were not distinguished for systematic theology. The bitter debates of the Reformation on salvation by faith and salvation by works did not disturb them, and the Anglican Thirty Nine

Heroes of the Slave Trade Abolition.
top: Sharp and Macaulay, *centre:* Wilberforce,
bottom: Buxton and Clarkson

Articles of Religion were ambiguous on the subject. The Sect were largely Calvinist, believing in salvation by faith alone of a predetermined "elect". The majority of reflective churchmen, and the followers of the Methodists, believed that Christ died for all, a doctrine reaffirmed by a Dutch theologian of the seventeenth century, Arminius. John Wesley's sermons and Charles Wesley's hymns ring with this Arminian faith.

A distinguished French historian later cast a sardonic eye over the English ecclesiastical landscape of that time. Of the Clapham Sect, he remarked on the strange paradox that men zealous for the dogma of justification by faith alone were "so devoted to philanthropy that on the common ground of good works they were reconciled with the most lukewarm Christians, even with the declared enemies of Christianity ... Never in the history of Anglicanism had any party exercised so profound an influence. Never had any party been in such a false position."[2]

French logic is not always a reliable theological tool and their faith was comprised in their vital piety, their unceasing practice in living the Christian life. In working for their chosen causes they accepted support from any source, from the Methodists always considered by William Wilberforce to be Churchmen, from Dissenters or, as we would now term them, Non-conformists. The most startling and quite uncharacteristic example of their ecumenism was James Stephen's confession to William Wilberforce in later life that he was "more than half a Roman Catholic." More understandable was their welcome of support from the dramatist Sheridan "drunk or sober" and from the dissolute Charles James Fox, the leading opposition politician and a fierce opponent of slavery. Politically they were nearly all Tories, but they followed an independent line, and as they formed a considerable body in the House of Commons, the Government was often anxious to secure their support.

Such were the politicians, professional and businessmen who founded the Sect. They were intelligent, influential and well-to-do, some very wealthy. They made their homes round the Common in considerable houses or mansions, enjoying each others companionship and co-operation in their good works. They lived a sociable, neighbourly almost communal life, happily flowing in and out of one another's houses, their children playing together in their pleasant gardens. They were united in their work, their beliefs. They nearly all worshipped together on Sundays at Holy Trinity Church on Clapham Common, which had been built in 1776.

Moreover, many of the Sect were related to one another. William Wilberforce and Henry Thornton were second cousins, Charles Elliott married John Venn's sister, Thomas Gisborne married Thomas Babington's sister and Babington married Zachary Macaulay's. James Stephen married Wilberforce's sister, his son James married a daughter of John Venn, Zachary Macaulay married a favourite pupil of Hannah More, the supply of sisters having run out.

Interior of Holy Trinity Church, drawn by J B Papworth in 1845, but as it was at the time of the Clapham Sect.
inset: John Venn.

The fight against slavery begins

Granville Sharp (1735–1813)

Granville Sharp was the patriarch of the Sect, and the first to take the field. He was grandson of an Archbishop of York, one of the fourteen children of the Archdeacon of Northumberland. Family funds having been exhausted, after a sketchy education he was apprenticed to a Quaker linen-draper on Tower Hill, but when his indenture was over he took an appointment in the Ordnance Office in the Tower. This he eventually lost when, in the War of American Independence (1776–83), his conscientious scruples unfortunately precluded his supplying arms to the British forces.

He was incurably quixotic and no windmill was safe from him; he had ardour of both heart and intellect; he studied Greek to dispute about the Trinity, Hebrew to argue with a Jew, and law to rescue the negro slaves who abounded in London, brought to this country by West Indian planter masters.

Granville Sharp found a wretched negro boy, Jonathan Strong, in his brother's City surgery, made so weak, blind and useless by savage treatment that his master had turned him out into the street. When the Sharp family had restored him to health, his master reclaimed him and tried to sell him to the Jamaican plantations. For two years Sharp studied and fought and eventually Jonathan Strong's freedom was secured, but on a procedural matter.

Other cases followed as Sharp battled against the finest lawyers of the day, including Lord Mansfield, the Lord Chief Justice, to get the legal position cleared satisfactorily. This he did in 1772 with the case of James

Somersett, a slave who had escaped, been recaptured and was being held captive in a ship on the Thames. Sharp applied to the courts for his release. Mansfield is usually given credit for his famous judgment which made slavery in Britain illegal, but in fact he was extremely reluctant to make such inroads into private property and to have about 14,000 negroes set free in England. He fought long and hard to prevent this but Granville Sharp gradually wore him down, "though poor, dependent and immersed in the duties of a toilsome calling". Granville Sharp had supplied "the money, the leisure, the perseverance and the learning needed for this great controversy".[3] But the famous words are Mansfield's: the state of slavery "is so odious that nothing can be suffered to support it, but positive law. Whatever inconveniences, therefore, may follow from the decision, I cannot say that this case is allowed or approved by the law of England, and therefore the black must be discharged." "As soon as a slave sets foot on English ground, he becomes free" in Sharp's words. Henceforth, though employed in many other crusades the attack on slavery was Granville Sharp's main object.

Until about the mid-eighteenth century, even in an age called the Enlightenment, slavery was almost universally accepted as an inevitable, if unpleasant, part of the structure of society, apparently approved of in the Bible, and in any case very profitable to traders and plantation owners. A hundred years later (sixty or eighty years in the case of Britain) slavery was abhorred by most thinking people in the Western world. We have here one of the great revolutions in human sympathies, ideas and beliefs. Slavery was no longer defended on Biblical grounds, but belief grew in a progressive Providence which revealed new truths and justified new practices, new ideas – a belief which Edmund Burke described as the "known march of the ordinary Providence of God." "Experience will decide" as an eighteenth century hymn put it. Many influential figures, Dr Johnson and John Wesley for example, roundly condemned slavery – in Wesley's words, "the execrable sum of all the villanies" – and it had become odious to many thinking people. Two factors, however, perpetuated it – the fear that the prosperity of the West Indies and of British traders depended on it, and the lack of conviction that anything could be done about it. Neither of these considerations meant anything to Granville Sharp.

The Quaker communities on both sides of the Atlantic had the honour of taking the first action and Sharp found here the support he needed. He wrote tracts, badgered bishops and when, in 1787, an Abolition Committee was formed he became its Chairman. The various groups working for the cause had a focal point and were formally consolidated into a fighting campaign, which included James Ramsay, vicar of Teston in Kent. He was a priest whose experience in the West Indies had made him burn with zeal to redress the wrongs of the negroes.

Granville Sharp rescues a slave.

inset: Thomas Clarkson.

His patron, Sir Charles Middleton (later Lord Barham), and Lady Middleton aided him in the cause. Another vital addition to the Committee was Thomas Clarkson.

Thomas Clarkson (1760–1846)

C LARKSON'S JOURNEY TO THIS POINT was by a strange route, and may be seen as a warning against writing essays. From St Paul's School he went to St John's College at Cambridge, and in 1784 the Vice-Chancellor, an opponent of slavery, set for the Latin essay prize of the University, "Is it lawful to make slaves of others against their will?" Clarkson won the prize and duly read his essay in the Senate House.

He left Cambridge planning to take Holy Orders, but as he rode along he began to be haunted by the arguments of his own essay and the conviction grew on him that if they were right, then "surely some person should interfere". He dismounted in his agitation and sat by the wayside to reconsider his whole future life: he then and there committed himself to work for the abolition of the slave trade.

In London he met Quakers who introduced him to Granville Sharp and he became an invaluable member of the Abolition Committee, its agent and fact-finder. Over the years he researched the slave trade by all possible means, poking about the sea-fronts of Bristol and Liverpool, collecting evidence about the ships, their conditions, buying specimens of shackles from sinister stores which supplied means of restraining or punishing the cargo.

He was in daily danger of his life from hostile traders of the 'West Indian interest'. The trade which was bloating these and other ports with riches was a triangular one – out to the West Coast of Africa with cheap goods and trinkets to supply the slaves' captors, mostly African or Arab, then laden with human cargo across the infamous Middle Passage to sell those who survived its horrors to the plantations in the West Indies and back to Britain with tobacco and sugar. The sugar trade especially was immensely profitable and heavily protected by the government.

Thomas Clarkson was indefatigable in his researches. One argument in favour of this abominable trade was that it was, in the phrase of the time, a "nursery of seamen". Clarkson produced precise evidence that the loss of life in the crews of the deadly slavery ships quite belied this belief. One piece of evidence which he sought could only be supplied by a seaman he had once seen but whose name he did not know. He found that sailor on the 317th ship he searched. He was skilful too in presenting his case. His famous engraving, a diagram of the negroes packed tightly between decks, based accurately on carefully collected measurements, made a great impression. Mrs More carried a copy with her to evening parties to horrify her fellow guests.

The Abolition Committee knew that the cause was ripe and looked for a leader who would take it up in Parliament, a man who "possessed the virtues of a fanatic without his vices".[4] He must persist and convince, have the intellect to master an intricate subject, have the necessary standing to command respect and have the attention of the Government. Clarkson set about securing the obvious choice – William Wilberforce. At Lady Middleton's suggestion Wilberforce was invited to Teston, and it was said at the time "The abolition of the slave trade was under God and when the time was come the work of a woman".[5]

Wilberforce himself counted this among the many impulses which directed him to the task which he was already contemplating. He had converse with Thomas Clarkson, with John Newton, with Granville Sharp and finally consulted his intimate friend, the Prime Minister, William Pitt. The tree in the Vale of Keston beneath which the friends sat is still shown. "Why don't you" said William Pitt "give notice of a motion on the subject of the Slave Trade?" Soon the political world knew that the Prime Minister's friend had taken the field in this cause. In 1789 William Wilberforce made his first speech on the subject in the House, the same year as the Bastille in Paris was stormed and the French Revolution began.

WILLIAM WILBERFORCE (1759–1833)

WILLIAM WILBERFORCE WAS THE SON of a wealthy Hull merchant in the Baltic trade, who died when William was a diminutive and frail child of ten, leaving him with a handsome fortune. To everyone's surprise, he survived childhood and went to Cambridge (St John's),

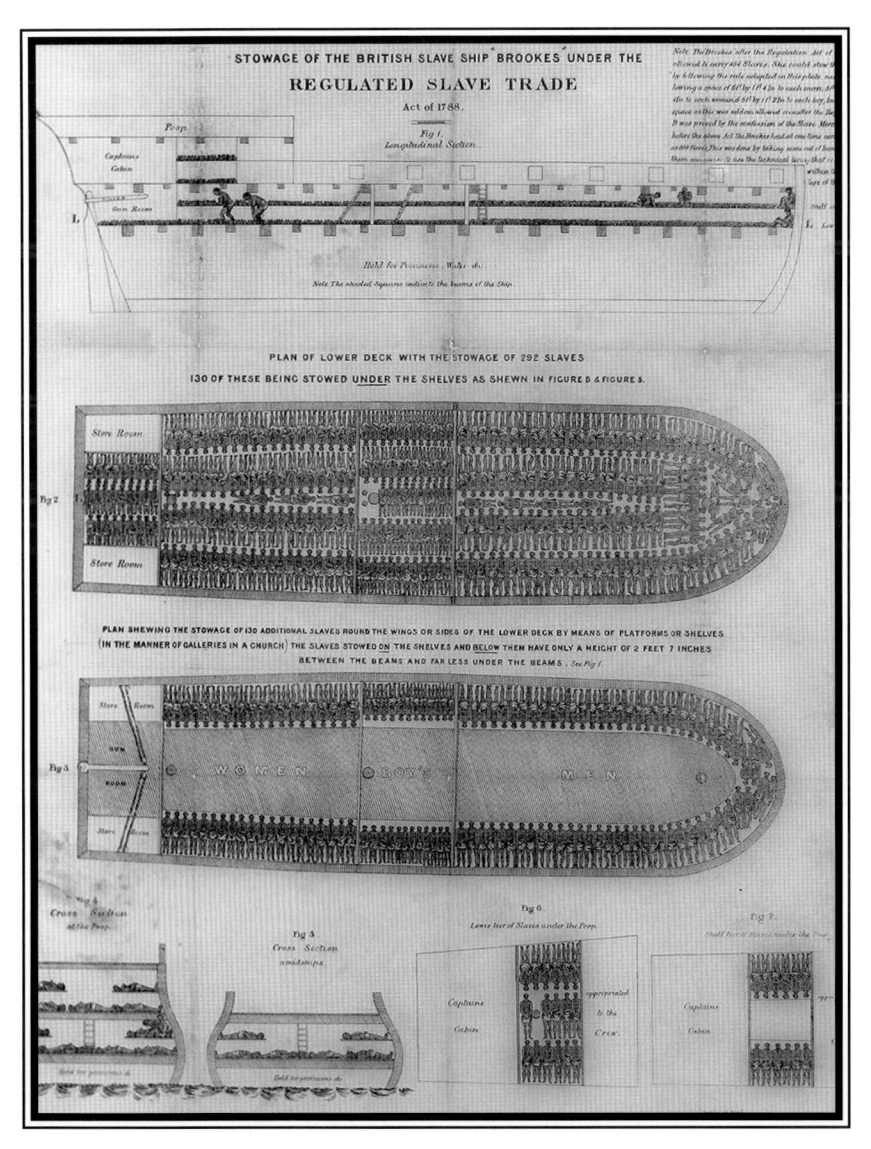

The slave ship *Brookes*:
an American version of the engraving
used by Clarkson and Mrs More.

William Wilberforce,
portrait by George Richmond.
1833.

where his friends were idle and the dons strove to make him idle. He did well in classics but neglected mathematics.

He then launched himself on a political career, becoming a Member of Parliament first for Hull and in 1784 one of the two Knights of the Shire for Yorkshire, the mightiest and most prestigious constituency. It was at the hustings in the courtyard of York Castle at the 1784 election that James Boswell heard the young Wilberforce speak. "I saw what seemed a mere shrimp mount upon the table; but as I listened he grew and grew until the shrimp became a whale". He was soon to become a parliamentary success, the "nightingale of the House",[6] adroit, quick-witted and eloquent in support of his friend and boon companion, William Pitt.

Wilberforce was not only enjoying his political career, he was having a fine time in the elegant gaiety of London society, dining with Charles James Fox, gambling with George Selwyn, supping with Mrs Siddons, dancing till dawn. He entertained everyone with his wit, charm and mercurial spirits. The death of an uncle left him richer still and possessor of a fine country villa at Wimbledon. If this was Vanity Fair, it was very agreeable, but William Wilberforce was hardly a Worldly Wiseman. It did not satisfy him and, just as his friend Pitt was soon to lose his youth in the responsibilities of being Prime Minister, his life was also to change.

Wilberforce invited Dr Isaac Milner, once his schoolmaster in Hull, now a powerful Cambridge Evangelical, to join him and his family on a foreign holiday. It was while travelling in one of the coaches alone with this companion studying Doddridge's *Rise and Progress of Religion* and the Greek testament, that by degrees their absorbing discussions began to convince him that he was not yet a 'Vital Christian'. The process of conversion was slow and sometimes very painful.

Back in London his former life-style became unbearable. He was rescued from excessive self-distrust and misery by the counsel of John Newton and the comfort of his Thornton relations and he gradually recovered his old cheerfulness. Of his new life-style he said "I will give it a more worthy epithet than gay. Let me call it serenity, tranquillity, composure which is not to be destroyed". His friends and family, observing his struggles, found with relief that what they feared was madness had passed.

"If this is madness," said a friend of his anxious mother, "I hope he will bite us all".

If historical events have an inside as well as an outside, then this is the inside of the events which gave Clapham its time of world importance.

Wilberforce returned to the House of Commons with a new conception of his political career. He became actively involved in the attempts to reform manners and morals through the Proclamation Society, so-called for its support of a Royal Proclamation against Vice and Immorality. This was supposed to reform the behaviour of the leaders of society. Inevitably, this resulted in criticising the behaviour of the poor and suppressing their amusements, whilst, as Sydney Smith said, "the gambling houses of St James's remain untouched". Wilberforce needed a wider and worthier field.

The approach of the Abolition Committee came at exactly the right time and subsequent events justify another historian[7] labelling this era as the Age of Wilberforce.

LET VS PRAISE GOD
FOR THE MEMORY AND EXAMPLE OF ALL THE FAITHFVLL
DEPARTED WHO HAVE WORSHIPPED IN THIS CHVRCH AND
ESPECIALLY FOR THE ABOVE NAMED
SERVANTS OF CHRIST SOMETIME CALLED·

THE CLAPHAM SECT
WHO IN THE LATTER PART OF THE XVIIITH AND EARLY PART
OF THE XIXTH CENTVRIES LABOVRED SO ABVNDANTLY FOR
NATIONAL RIGHTEOVSNESS AND THE CONVERSION OF THE
HEATHEN AND RESTED NOT VNTIL THE CVRSE OF SLAVERY
WAS SWEPT AWAY FROM ALL PARTS OF THE BRITISH DOMINIONS

CHARLES GRANT   HENRY THORNTON
ZACHARY MACAVLAY   JOHN THORNTON
GRANVILLE SHARP   HENRY VENN *Curate of Clapham*
JOHN SHORE *and Teignmouth*   JOHN VENN *Rector of Clapham*
JAMES STEPHEN   WILLIAM WILBERFORCE

*O God we have heard with our ears and our fathers have declared unto
us the noble works that Thou didst in their days and in the old time before them*

The plaque on the south wall
of Holy Trinity Church.
Damaged by enemy action in 1945.

[22]

The friends come to Clapham

The Thornton Family

So far Clapham can claim little share in these events, but it was preparing for its time of glory. The Thornton family is the key to this stage. They were a Yorkshire merchant family related to Wilberforce and again there is a connection with the Hull and Russia trade.

Robert (1692–1748) moved to London and in 1735 bought his country estate on the South Side of Clapham Common, land now occupied by St Mary's School and the Notre Dame Estate. His son, John (1720–90), also a Russia merchant and like his father a director of the Bank of England, greatly improved the estate which held several substantial houses.

John, a bit of a rough diamond, became the great financial supporter of the evangelical cause. He bought up advowsons (the right to appoint clergy to a parish) Clapham amongst them, in order to present livings to clergy of that persuasion, and he was active in the building of the new church, Holy Trinity, on the Common in 1776. Under the terms of his will, this living was presented in 1792 to John Venn, the son of Henry, who had been curate in Clapham.

John Venn (1759–1833)

John Venn was highly intelligent, diffident, affectionate, and above all, a man of prudent and practical zeal. When he was offered this living his father and like-minded friends had difficulty in persuading him to accept the challenge. Clapham was a great contrast to the quiet Norfolk village where he had previously served. It was the most rapidly growing village around London, its Common drained and planted, its roads improved, it was already inhabited by substantial citizens such as the Thorntons.

Venn became first and foremost Rector of a parish undergoing rapid social and economic change and beset with war-time problems. There were many poor and needy and children in want of education. Carefully distinguishing between the deserving and the undeserving poor, Venn transformed Clapham into a mini-welfare state. He divided it into districts with committees of tea-drinking ladies, distributing food, clothing, blankets, medicines and most unusually administering effective means of preventing the spread of epidemics by fumigation, disinfection and isolation. In 1800, Venn introduced the new vaccination against smallpox to his flock.

This Clapham Poor Society was in addition to the efficient discharge of its legal obligation by the Parish Vestry under the Poor Laws. John Venn was active in the parish schools (now represented by Macaulay School) and he provided special teaching services in church for children and young people and their parents. He installed the chandelier in the new church to enable him to have Sunday evening teaching services for them. This caused trouble. A card club which met at The Plough (the main posting inn in Clapham) on Sunday evenings considered that he was putting on a rival attraction and moreover probably spreading French Revolutionary subversive ideas. Venn was also active in forming the Home Guard of the day, the Clapham Armed Association, in 1798 to repel Napoleon's threat of invasion. Venn, in fact, was an early example of the 'town parsons' so active in the nineteenth century.

When John Venn took up residence in 1793, John Thornton was dead, and his sons Samuel and Robert were living on South Side. Samuel later set up as a country gentleman, and Robert aspired to fashionable life, entertained royalty in his elegant Orangery, still standing in the Notre Dame Estate, and later had to flee to America to escape his creditors.

Venn knew at the outset of his ministry that they and fellow parishioners would not welcome enthusiasm and he began his preaching with some caution. This changed when Henry Thornton, the youngest brother, a businessman-banker, and MP for Southwark from 1782, moved from the City to the delightful Queen Anne house on the West Side of the

The Thornton family *of Birkin*
|
John Thornton *of Kingston-upon-Hull*

Robert Thornton 1692-1748 = Hannah Swynocke

Sarah = William Wilberforce

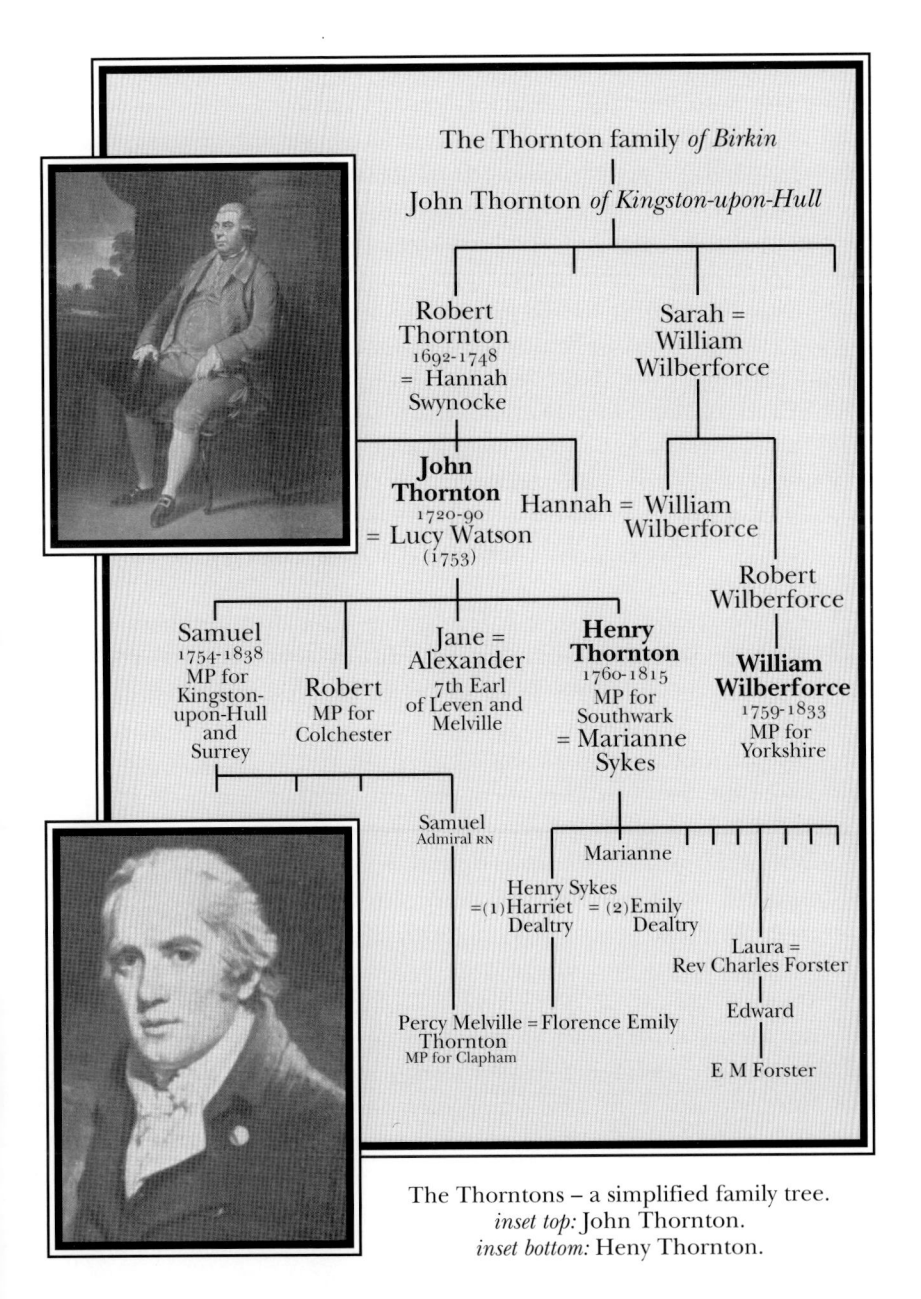

John Thornton 1720-90 = Lucy Watson (1753)

Hannah = William Wilberforce

Robert Wilberforce

Samuel 1754-1838 MP for Kingston-upon-Hull and Surrey

Robert MP for Colchester

Jane = Alexander 7th Earl of Leven and Melville

Henry Thornton 1760-1815 MP for Southwark = Marianne Sykes

William Wilberforce 1759-1833 MP for Yorkshire

Samuel Admiral RN

Marianne

Henry Sykes =(1)Harriet = (2)Emily
Dealtry   Dealtry

Laura = Rev Charles Forster

Percy Melville = Florence Emily Thornton
MP for Clapham

Edward
|
E M Forster

The Thorntons – a simplified family tree.
inset top: John Thornton.
inset bottom: Heny Thornton.

[25]

Common, Battersea Rise House. He invited his cousin William Wilberforce to share his bachelor home, and together they welcomed and encouraged Venn's beliefs. Gradually Venn established his reputation as an excellent preacher of evangelical doctrines.

The church and its galleries were nearly always full, two new beadles had to be appointed to control the parking problem (Holy Trinity has the staves provided for their use and the schedule of their duties). A porch was added to the West End to protect folk alighting from their carriages, and speaking tubes were installed to enable select members of the congregation to listen to the service and sermon (long) from the comfort and privacy of the vestry. The pulpit was then in the middle of the East End, quite overshadowing the beautiful Chippendale communion table presented by a North Side banker.

HENRY THORNTON (1760–1815)

SUCH WAS THE PARISH AND VILLAGE to which the members of the Clapham Sect gathered. Charles Elliott moved from the City to Grove House in Old Town to be in his brother-in-law's parish and the bonding of the Sect may be said to have begun when Battersea Rise House became the joint home of Henry Thornton and William Wilberforce. It became the Sect's headquarters, and its new oval library designed by Pitt its operations centre.

When Henry Thornton married, Wilberforce moved into Broomwood House, formerly Edward Eliot's home, in the Thornton grounds. If Wilberforce was the star, Henry Thornton should be considered the nucleus of the fraternity.

Bankers are not usually given to flights of fancy, and imagination was not Henry's forte. But his practical sagacity and his probity made him a most successful and trusted man of business and his intelligence gave him a grasp of the abstract problems of finance. He wrote a classic *Enquiry into Paper Credit.* His fortune was handsome, though not splendid and he judged that it ought never to be "increased by accumulation nor diminished by sumptuousness".[8] Before his marriage he gave away six-sevenths of his income; after that as head of a growing family (six daughters and three sons) he gave at least one-third of it.

His calm judicial and persevering shrewdness was exactly the quality which enabled the Clapham Sect to maximise its strengths and its achievements. Clapham attracted other members of the Sect like a magnet, and the very lay-out of the village, with houses and mansions ranged round the Common, contributed to their close collaboration.

CHARLES GRANT (1746–1823)

CHARLES GRANT BUILT HIS HOUSE, GLENELG, in the very grounds of Battersea Rise House. He was a Scot, who added a rare note of romance to the Sect's story, for he was named after Bonnie Prince Charlie in whose cause his father had perished.

Charles's guardians sent him in 1769 to India to make his fortune, which he duly did, but rather unusually by honest means. In the service of the East India Company he eventually had charge of all the trade of Bengal. Family tragedy brought about his conversion to Christianity, and in 1790 he returned to England for the sake of his wife's health and to urge the toleration and establishment of Christian missions in India, which it was the policy of the East India Company to prevent.

It was at this stage that he met John Venn who undertook the education of his two sons in his Norfolk parsonage. Grant never returned to India but worked on the East India Company's Court of Directors, eventually, as Director of the Directors, ruling India from Leadenhall Street. To move to Clapham as the neighbour of Wilberforce and the parishioner of Venn seemed almost inevitable.

JOHN SHORE, LORD TEIGNMOUTH (1751–1834)

IN 1802 CHARLES GRANT WAS RESPONSIBLE for introducing John Shore, Lord Teignmouth, to Wilberforce. He had been Governor-General of India, a quiet, useful, wholly honest man who chose his abode by the quality of the neighbours. Samuel Thornton now having set himself up with a country seat, Shore moved into his house on a site now occupied by St Mary's Church.

[27]

As one who knew him well wrote it must ever remain "one of the dark problems of parochial history" that "the quiet, everyday gentleman who was to be seen walking with his children on Clapham Common" or sitting on the Clapham coach had ruled the East like Aurangzebe, the last of the Mogul Emperors, had been an associate of Warren Hastings, had had "hair-breadth escapes and strange Adventures".[9] His membership of the Sect brought it no pomp and circumstance, but quiet, useful service.

JAMES STEPHEN (1758–1832)

CHARLES GRANT AND JOHN SHORE gave an Indian dimension to the Sect's labours. Two other members had direct experience of West Indian conditions. James Stephen came from a family of Scottish small farmers and merchants, and had struggled to secure a legal education. He successfully practised in the West Indies, and married later after some somewhat colourful complications.

He visited England in 1788-89 and sought out William Wilberforce because he was passionately committed to the anti-slavery cause, having witnessed in Barbados a slave being burnt alive after a travesty of a trial. He then helped the cause by supplying it with clandestine information.

When he finally returned to England in 1794 he settled in Clapham to be near the Sect, and, his first wife having died, he married Wilberforce's sister. His legal career in England was distinguished, he rose to be a Master in Chancery, and entered Parliament. A fiery and passionate advocate of Abolition, James Stephen was inclined to blame Wilberforce for giving his time to anything else, and more temperate colleagues had some difficulty in restraining his terrible temper.

ZACHARY MACAULAY (1768–1838)

THE OTHER 'WEST INDIAN' MEMBER OF THE SECT was a man of very different stamp, Zachary Macaulay. He came from a long line of Scots ministers and had been sent, as a mere lad, to be overseer on a Jamaican estate – he thus had first hand experience of the plantation system. He tried to carry on his work as humanely as possible, but when he returned

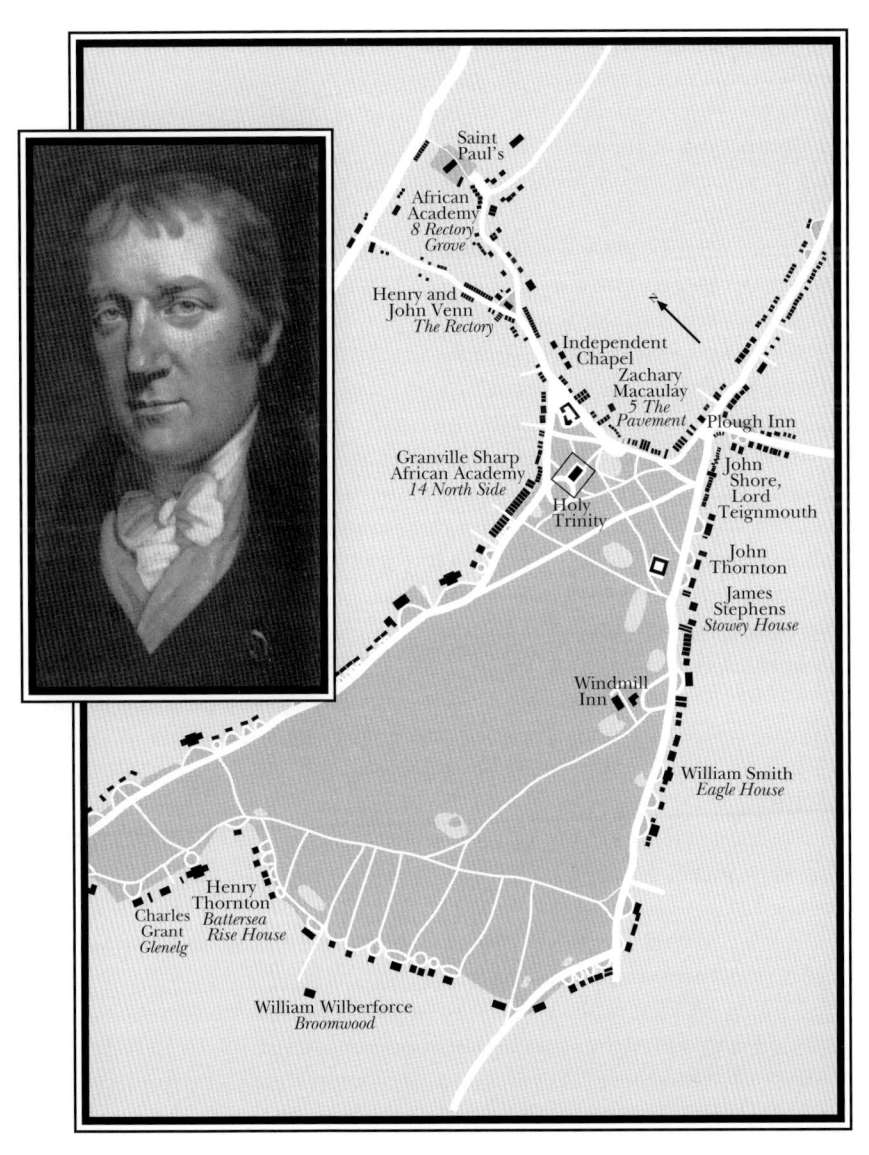

Map of Clapham Common
based on map of 1815.
inset: William Smith.

to England to visit a sister who had married Thomas Babington he realised that compromise with such evil was impossible.

This reserved, austere, dogged young Scot was to become the encyclopaedia of the Sect ("look it up in Macaulay" they said), but first he was to be the link with the patriarch and pioneer of the campaign, Granville Sharp.

Lord Mansfield's apprehensions of the result of his famous judgment (page 15) were justified. The freeing of about 14,000 black slaves in England led to problems which were intensified by the demobilisation in 1783 of negroes who had fought for the British side in the American War of Independence.

Granville Sharp supported many destitute negroes from his own slender means. In 1786 a suggestion of forming a settlement in Africa was eagerly taken up, land in Sierra Leone and government funds were secured and in 1787 the first consignment of negroes was taken out. What followed was an epic of disaster – the settlers, mostly quite unprepared and unsuited for the life, were often mutinous and idle, or melted into the bush. The climate was unhealthy, and a consignment of London prostitutes had somehow been included in the party. Nearby slaving depots were naturally hostile, and so were the local chiefs. When war with France was declared the French navy took its turn to burn and sack the settlement. Fire gutted the supply ships, and there were incredible swarms of ants.

A series of governors struggled with these disasters and difficulties, the most successful being Thomas Clarkson's naval brother. In 1791 the Sierra Leone Company was incorporated by Act of Parliament with Granville Sharp as President, Henry Thornton Chairman, Charles Grant and Wilberforce among its directors.

Young Zachary Macaulay was appointed Second Member in the Council and sailed for Africa. He soon succeeded to the position and duties of Governor. All was on his shoulders – administration, finance, justice, even the duties of a chaplain. His dogged courage and abilities survived even the pillaging and burning of the settlement by French Jacobin soldiers and sailors under the captaincy of an American slaver.

In 1795 after a short recuperation in England during which he became engaged to Selina Mills, Mrs More's pupil, he was back at his post. The tide began to turn. The settlers learnt from the last attack and began to co-operate, agriculture and trade increased, the capital, Freetown, grew to a substantial and quite profitable settlement. The Sierra Leone Company became the first of the Chartered Companies, and then in 1808 Sierra Leone was made a Crown Colony. It played an important part in the settling of liberated slaves during the next century.

Macaulay returned to England in 1799, and married his Selina. He brought a number of African children to be educated as future leaders of Sierra Leone and established a school for them at 8 Rectory Grove. The school later moved to 14 North Side, but few of the children survived our climate.

Zachary and his family moved into 5 The Pavement (now Evans' shop) and it was here that little Tom Macaulay, later to become Lord Macaulay, once entertained Mrs Hannah More with the offer of a glass of old spirits, suggested to him as suitable hospitality for an elderly lady of devout habits by his reading of *Robinson Crusoe*.

Granville Sharp in old age

Granville Sharp, the first in the cause, was perhaps the last of the Sect to settle in Clapham. He was for most of his life a City man and he must have been old when he came to live at 14 Clapham Common North Side.

He still worked eagerly, not only to abolish the trade in slaves, but for their liberation. The other members of the Sect realised that immediate pursuit of this greatest good would have prevented any good being achieved. This wise prudence was not in Sharp's style, but was an important factor in the Sect's success, too often ignored in popular histories.

In old age Sharp, as valuable a worker as ever, was something of a beloved eccentric. He was more and more inclined to lose himself in obscure biblical prophecies – he once tried to convince Charles James Fox that Napoleon was the Little Horn of the Old Testament Book of Daniel. "The Little Horn, Mr Sharp, the Little Horn?" replied the bewildered Whig leader, "and what in the name of wonder do you mean by the Little Horn?" To poor Sharp, "That man passes for a statesman, and yet it is evident to me that he never so much as heard of the Little Horn".

WILLIAM SMITH (1756–1835)

THE NAMES OF THE SECT ON THE TABLET on the south wall of Holy Trinity have now been assembled – Charles Grant, Zachary Macaulay, Granville Sharp, John Shore, James Stephen, Henry and John Thornton, Henry and John Venn, William Wilberforce, (Thomas Clarkson was never resident). It is not surprising that Venn, a modest man, should have hesitated in accepting a parish containing men of such formidable distinction.

One name, however, is missing; William Smith was a Non-conformist and later a Unitarian (who did not believe in the Trinity). Because he was in some sense the 'odd man out' in the Sect it is worth looking at his career a bit more closely. He came from a prosperous City family of retail grocers. His father made his country house in Clapham, and Smith, like Thornton, can be called a native of this Holy Village, which had one of the oldest meeting places of the Independents, the Chapel represented until its closure in 2002 by the United Reformed Church in Grafton Square.

On the advice of its Minister, the Reverend Philip Furneaux, young Smith, already well grounded at a dissenting school (at Ware), was sent in 1769 to the dissenting academy at Daventry, one of the best of these colleges, where as their historian has claimed,[10] modern education was born. For the education of future ministers and for lay youths, the three learned languages, Latin, Greek and Hebrew, were studied, also modern languages, natural philosophy (that is, several branches of science) mathematics, civil government and "Evidences and Moral Duties of Christians". This was a much wider course than he would have followed at the universities, from which as a Dissenter, he was excluded.

For nine years after leaving Daventry William Smith worked in his father's counting house, but he looked to a political career. He married and settled down in the handsome and spacious Eagle House on the South Side of the Common where he and his wife Frances lived an elegant and cultivated life and raised a large family (the eighth, Octavius, was born in 1794 and there were still two more to come). He began to build up a fine collection of paintings which eventually became a nucleus of the National Gallery, and each year lengthy and arduous tours were made (babies included) to picturesque regions such as the Lake District.

Smith was one of the few members of the Sect to show any aesthetic leanings. He entered Parliament in 1784, the year in which Wilberforce was elected for Yorkshire and which established William Pitt in office with an adequate majority. The laws which excluded Dissenters from office had largely fallen into disuse, that is for those wealthy enough, and Smith was quite rich enough to buy Sudbury which had an electorate of 800 freemen, a rotten rather than a pocket borough. Parliamentary reform was becoming one of the causes of the day and one to which Smith, a Whig, was seriously committed, but in the meantime it was necessary to play the system.

From 1802 to 1806 and from 1807 to 1830 Smith was Member for Norwich, a city with one of the largest electorates in the country and a radical tradition. His parliamentary career became increasingly liberal, even radical, and he fought tirelessly for the reform of Parliament, the freeing of Dissenters from the disabilities of the seventeenth century laws which excluded them from public life, for freedom of the press, for freedom of worship and belief, for peace with France, for the abolition of the slave trade.

He left Clapham in 1794 to live more in the centre of Whig politics but he remained an intimate and beloved member of the Sect. He was with Wilberforce and his friends when they celebrated the final victory in 1807 and it was in his house in Cadogan Place that Wilberforce died.

The most vivid contemporary picture of the happy life-style of the Clapham brotherhood includes William Smith. James Stephen the younger, writing in 1843, recalled the scene "some forty summers ago" when the "usual group" of all ages and various families was assembled in the oval library at Battersea Rise House where he himself sat reading a book. The busy hum of voices and activities was suspended "to welcome the approach of what seemed a dramatic procession emerging from the shrubbery which marked, but not divided, the garden from its neighbour: a couple of "urchins" (one of them the future Bishop of Oxford), a large shaggy dog, an assortment of constituents, petitioners, supporters and the frail darting figure of Wilberforce, his pockets bulging like saddle-bags, one hand waving a book, the other grasping a spade. This in turn he waved like a wand, brandished like a truncheon or used like a cutlass to threaten "the robust form of William Smith, who as commodore of this ill-assorted squadron, was endeavouring to convey them to their destined port" – no easy task when Wilberforce moved "in obedience to some impulse like that which prompts the wheeling of a swallow" his "rich voice ranging over all the chords expressive of mirth, of tenderness, of curiosity or surprise, of delight or of indignation".

Nurse Hunter and the assembled family
in the famous Library at Battersea Rise,
by Henrietta Thornton, circa 1825.

Christian mission

Australia

THE SCENE SET, THE CAST ASSEMBLED, the action must continue. The Sect fought so many campaigns, and supported so many philanthropic causes that it is important to remember that always their principal purpose was the spread of a particular version of the Christian Gospel, for this secured not only temporal help but eternal bliss. They started briskly and the first move places Clapham firmly on a world stage.

In 1786 Wilberforce learned that the first consignment of convicts to be dumped in Botany Bay was ready to sail – the former American colonies being no longer available for such purpose. He and Thornton hastened to Pitt, arranged the appointment of a chaplain, secured someone ready to go, and the Gospel was thus carried to Australia.

India

INDIA WAS NOT TO BE DEALT WITH IN SUCH A BRISK STYLE. Charles Grant returned from India in 1790 with the purpose of getting the East India Company to support missions not only as chaplains to its own servants, many of them in sore need of them, but to the Indians. The renewal of the Company's charter gave an opportunity for action.

But the Company did not consider that it had any obligations to the native population – its purpose was trade. It had great respect for the ancient civilisation of India and if its beliefs tolerated such unfortunate practices as burning widows alive that was their affair. In turn, the behaviour of many of the Company's servants secured little respect for the religion of Europeans. Grant spent his last years in India in careful, but not very profitable, moves to secure missionary work and sent home to Wilberforce and others a Proposal for a mission sanctioned by the civil government. This came to nothing.

When he returned to England he was soon breakfasting with Wilberforce, meeting Thornton, and in 1794 moved out to Clapham a fully paid-up member of the Sect, one might say. Wilberforce had hopes that when in 1793 the Company charter was renewed provision would be made, but "like a giant aroused from sleep India House began to stir".[11] The idea of its preserves being invaded by enthusiasts concerned with the welfare of the natives brought forth all its strengths and resources. From the gallery of the Commons, Grant had to watch the defeat of Wilberforce's modest proposals.

THE CHURCH MISSIONARY SOCIETY

BUT THE CLAPHAMITES WERE NOT YET DEFEATED and history was on their side. By 1800, despite its origins, Christianity had become almost exclusively a European religion, and it was far from certain that it would be successful in turning itself into a universal religion. Yet by the year 2000, most Christians lived outside Western Europe. An historian (Professor Keith Robbins) could claim that the new millennium appears likely to be one in which the centre of gravity in Christianity shifts away from a European-centred tradition, and could refer to his experience of worshipping in an "Anglican church in a Moslem country ... in a packed congregation consisting of people of Indian and Chinese descent" and finding himself with the British High Commissioner, "the sole representative of Western Christianity".[12] In the transition from a European to a world religion, the Clapham Sect played a vital part.

The Baptists founded the first of the missionary societies which spearheaded this change, then came the London Missionary Society in 1795, not tied to any particular denomination but in fact becoming largely Independent (or Congregationalist). To John Venn and his colleagues this was a challenge indeed. He and his fellow evangelical clergy in and around London used to meet regularly for fellowship and discussion in the Eclectic Society at the Castle and Falcon Inn in Aldersgate Street. At their meeting on 18 March 1799 Venn introduced the debate on "What method can we use more effectively to promote the knowledge of the Gospel among the heathen?" Soon they were deciding how to found a society "on the Church principle, but not the High Church principle"; that is, how it could be kept in evangelical hands and yet under episcopal governance – there must be nothing "irregular".

This Society for Missions in Africa and the East was later renamed the Church Missionary Society and fittingly celebrated its bicentenary in a huge tent on Clapham Common in 1999 – for the Sect rallied stalwartly behind its Rector. Charles Elliott was, with his brother-in-law John Venn, at the founding meeting; Charles Grant, William Wilberforce, James Stephen were Vice-Presidents. Henry Thornton was the treasurer, Thomas Babington on the Committee and Zachary Macaulay joined when he returned to England. Venn was Chairman and his prayer in the Society's prospectus linked it with the best known of Clapham's crusades:
> "They pray that while every country brings its stores to Great Britain she may return to them treasures more valuable than silver and gold. They trust that the wrongs which Africa has so long sustained will at length be repaired by the offerings of spiritual peace and Christian freedom".[13]

Appropriately one of the panels in the east window at Holy Trinity Church shows Venn, kindly supported by St Paul, offering the missionary cause to the Trinity in the centre panel.

It was fortunate that one of Venn's principles was to begin on a small scale, "colonies creep from small beginnings". It took the Archbishop of Canterbury a year to give a cautious response – he "could not with propriety at once express his full concurrence and approbation". But the Society set about recruiting missionaries, and found that the very concept of such a vocation had to be created and fostered. The first sent out to Africa were German Lutherans.

The difficulty of getting any missionaries to India seemed insuperable. Even when John Shore became Governor-General he could do little. In the end Charles Grant managed to get Henry Martyn, a Cambridge Evangelical who translated the scriptures and Prayer Book into Indian native languages, there as Chaplain to the Company, and gradually further suitable men were sent in this capacity.

The East India Company's Charter had to be renewed once more in 1813 and in good time a huge campaign of parliamentary petitions, pamphlets, lobbying, meetings, interviews (Wilberforce's specialty) was mounted. The Church Missionary Society anniversary rally was dedicated to the cause of establishing bishops in India. But the parliamentary victory was due not so much to all these preparations or Wilberforce's oratory as to the petitions which poured in from all over the country, 837 of them bearing more than half a million signatures.

The Sect and its allies had marshalled a new force, and brought into being a new kind of politics. When the Bill passed its final reading Wilberforce, Stephen, Babington, Thornton, Grant (now MP for Inverness-shire) and his son Charles all contributed to the debate and the final victory. The first grant for Indian education was made and an episcopal establishment secured for India.

The South London Press reported the 200th anniversary of CMS at Holy Trinity, May 1999.
inset: Hannah More.

MISSION AT HOME

CLAPHAM WAS ALSO CONCERNED WITH MISSIONS AT HOME, and the Sect engaged in education and propaganda on every possible front. They supported Sunday schools, already a widely flourishing movement teaching children on the only day when they were not at work. Reading, and occasionally writing (for boys only) were the staple diet. The early day schools for the poor were supported through two pioneer societies, the interdenominational British and Foreign School Society of the Quaker, Joseph Lancaster, in which William Smith was active, and the Anglican National Society of the Reverend Andrew Bell. Both these used the 'monitorial' system in which older and more advanced pupils taught the others.

Venn rejoiced that every child in Clapham could learn to read. Wilberforce was the instigator of the schools of the More sisters in the Mendips, and he and Thornton helped to finance them. These early movements for 'popular education', although their main purpose was to enable children to read the Bible, much alarmed many of the governing classes – they would make the workers discontented with their lot, uncivil to their betters, and enable them to read subversive literature (Tom Paine *et al.*). But Wilberforce in the House of Commons declared that "if people were destined to be free, they must be made fit to enjoy their freedom".

Moreover, the Clapham Sect and like-minded folk set about providing suitable and safe reading material for them, and discovered a great appetite for reading in the humblest places. Today the distribution of religious tracts to the 'lower orders' does not usually have a good press, especially among the politically correct. But Mrs More's wit and sparkle made a great success of such tracts and found an eager market.

The Clapham Sect helped Mrs More to organise periodical production and distribution of what were called (most unappealingly) Cheap Repository Tracts. Depots for their sale were set up and the hawkers and peddlers were also pressed into service, Thornton having made a special study of their habits. Nearly two million tracts were sold in the first year and while some of these were bought for free distribution, most were bought by the newly literate. From this grew the Religious Tract Society, not one of the Clapham Sect's initiatives, but substantially supported by them, with contributions, money, practical experience. They also indirectly supplied the Society's most prolific writer, the newly converted Legh Richmond, whose tract *The Dairyman's Daughter* sold two million copies.

This timely conversion was the result of Legh Richmond's reading Wilberforce's *Practical View of the Prevailing System of Professed Christians in the Higher and Middle Classes in the Country Contrasted with the Real Christianity* (1797). This daunting title explains exactly the purpose of the work – it was not only the lower orders who needed improving reading. A cautious publisher ventured on 500 copies and was amazed at its immediate success – 7,500 copies in six months; by 1826 fifteen editions had appeared in England, twenty-five in America, and translations into French, Dutch, Italian, Spanish and German had been made. This onslaught on the wealthy was of vital importance if society was to be transformed.

John Wesley had brought the message to the humble and modest, but recognised that his very success there kept the well-to-do and socially aspiring away from his teaching. Mrs More's *Thoughts on the Importance of Manners of the Great to General Society* (1788) had brought her a message from Wesley telling her to continue her work in reforming the rich "for they will not let us come nigh them". In 1790 when the great and the fashionable were quaking at the news from revolutionary France, Mrs More followed up her first attack with a scathing *Estimate of the Religion of the Fashionable World*.

Wilberforce in his *Practical View* was building on these foundations and his immense popularity and the almost universal confidence in his integrity and sincerity made his entry into the lists of great importance. He himself said that he knew his vocation was two-fold – the abolition of the slave trade and the "reformation of manners".

The reform of social leaders was strategically vital, but success depended on the solid support of the middle ranks of society. For them, from 1792, *The Christian Observer* was provided, a monthly periodical costing one shilling, much less than other magazines. Venn's prospectus described it as "a review of religion, literature and politics such as a clergyman may without scruple commend to his parishioners and a Christian safely introduce into his family".

Josiah Pratt of the Eclectic Society was the first editor, but he was soon replaced by Macaulay, who for fourteen years carried out this laborious duty. It was a lasting success, especially as Wilberforce kept a lively eye on it, asking Mrs More to contribute something sparkling to what he feared was too heavy: "If it is not enlivened it will sink". Members of the Sect contributed many articles, Thornton eighty-three articles between 1802 and 1815, and Macaulay himself wrote regularly.

From its first number until 1845, *The Christian Observer* was published by John Hatchard whose bookshop still flourishes in Piccadilly. He moved from over the shop in 1821 to Stonely House in Clapham, close to Wix's Lane on the north side of the Common, perhaps because his beliefs and life-style accorded with those of the Sect, who had long used his bookshop as a club and for anti-slavery meetings – Wilberforce had his mail delivered there.

THE BIBLE SOCIETY

IN 1802 A METHODIST MINISTER FROM WALES wrote to the Religious Tract Society deploring the scarcity of Bibles in Wales. Mr Hughes, the Baptist Minister from Battersea, responded vigorously: "A society might be formed for the purpose" of providing Bibles not only for Wales, "why not for the kingdom, why not for the whole world?" The carrying out of this proposal needed experience and influence, and eyes very naturally turned towards Clapham. So was the British and Foreign Bible Society born. The counting-house of a Methodist businessman, Joseph Hardcastle, of Clapham, and Wilberforce's breakfast table saw the plans develop. The Society was to supply and distribute the Scriptures in as many languages as possible, without comment.

The public meeting which launched the Society was held on 7 March 1804, Granville Sharp was in the Chair, and the Clapham Sect was in full support – William Wilberforce, Thomas Babington, Charles Grant, Zachary Macaulay, James Stephen and later Charles Elliott were on the Committee; Granville Sharp, Thomas Gisborne and William Dealtry (later Rector of Clapham) were made Honorary Governors for life. Lord Teignmouth was shortly asked to be President and became a devoted worker for the Society, declaring he "would be content to be forgotten as Governor-General of India, if only he might be remembered as President of the Bible Society".

In the first five years the Society distributed 150,000 Bibles, in the second five years, 800,000, and promoted its translation in whole or in part into 140 languages – some of the early translations had to be later replaced by more satisfactory attempts. The Society had little official support from the Established Church, unhappy with its interdenominational character, and perhaps with the degree of organised lay support, especially of women's associations. These auxiliary societies sprang up all over the country almost spontaneously, demonstrating that public opinion was strongly behind the endeavour. The auxiliary for Clapham and its neighbourhood was founded at a meeting in Kennington in 1812; Samuel Thornton was its President. The Society and its work marked "an important epoch in the religious history of mankind".[14]

Church Mission settlement at Bathurst,
in Sierra Leone.
Nineteenth century.

Abolition of the slave trade

A LL THESE MULTIFARIOUS PHILANTHROPIES and many more were taken up by men already engaged in professional and public work. James Stephen was a busy lawyer and MP, Henry Thornton a banker and MP for Southwark, Charles Grant an MP and busy governing India from the City, William Wilberforce MP for Yorkshire. Above all the Sect was tenaciously persevering with the greatest crusade of all – to abolish the slave trade. Wilberforce had made his first abolition speech in the House in 1789, but success did not come till 1807.

The struggle was inevitably hard and long. The West Indian and sugar refining interest was entrenched and powerful and usually quite unscrupulous. Respect for property, even in human flesh, was embedded in the social thinking of the times. It was strengthened and protected by the panic fear aroused by the French Revolution. And this fear was not altogether imaginary. The Terror in France was horrible enough and the ugly, terrifying memory of the slave revolt in the French island of St Dominique in 1791, where slaves had taken the revolutionary doctrines of the *Rights of Man* too literally, had turned that beautiful and fertile island into a hell on earth. The mildest suggestion for relieving the plight of chimney-sweeps' climbing boys tended to be seen as a Jacobin plot. From 1794 there began the long and desperate wars with France.

The political situation complicated matters further. William Pitt was a steadfast supporter of abolition, but his party was deeply divided on the issue and even its so-called supporters were often half-hearted or prevaricatory, suggesting regulation of the trade, or postponement of the decision. The Whig opposition was largely abolitionist but not to be relied upon to support the war effort. To make matters worse the king,

George III, was obstinately opposed to abolition and his sanity was precarious, especially if he were thwarted. If a regency became necessary, the Prince of Wales was thought to be Whig in sympathy and likely to replace Pitt with Charles James Fox who had hailed the French Revolution with ardent delight. Pitt was treading a political tightrope and often the Clapham friends meeting for their Cabinet Councils in the Oval Library must have despaired of his procrastinations and manoeuvres. The fiery James Stephen even tried to quarrel with Wilberforce for making allowances for Pitt's predicament.

For eighteen years from 1789, while the fate of Europe hung in the balance, the frail little figure of Wilberforce rose almost annually in the House to plead with masterly eloquence, supported by varied, precise, well presented evidence, for the cause of the slaves. Even the apparently indefatigable Clarkson broke down under the stress of his labours and for nine years quitted the battle-field.

Pitt, his health ebbing away, lived to rejoice and mourn at the news of Trafalgar (1805) but died in the following year with the disaster of

"The Plumb-pudding in Danger – or – State Epicures taking un Petit Souper."
James Gillray's cartoon of Pitt and Napoleon
dividing the world, 1805.

Austerlitz (1806). His "Roll up that map, it will not be wanted this ten years" has made the *Oxford Dictionary of Quotations*. Britannia ruled the waves, but Napoleon was master of Europe. Fox, after brief office, died in the same year with only time to secure a measure to curb the trade.

It became clear however that the many years of bitter frustration had been well used. Public opinion had been instructed, rallied and marshalled by the labours and all the resources of the Sect and their allies. "From the moment the British people had been fully and authoritatively informed of the black truth about the Trade, Abolition sooner or later was certain".[15]

The meetings, rallies, pamphlets, petitions (presented with masterly timing), the household campaign to ban the use of West Indian sugar, had done their work and now at last the time was ripe. Political, economic and strategic factors briefly converged to make a unique parliamentary opportunity. With superb teamwork, the abolitionists went into action. William Smith rallied the Whig co-operation, the wily Stephen, fortified by the Gospel advice to be as wise as serpents, urged the strategy of keeping arguments of humanity and justice in a low key and basing the case for abolition on consideration of national interest. The first stage of abolition, in 1806, was secured by this policy. The final stage included more open pleas for justice to produce in the House what Wilberforce called a "fit of heroism". The slave trade was finally outlawed on 1 May 1807.

Fox had died before the task was finished. Grenville, who had sat with Wilberforce and Pitt beneath that tree in the Vale of Keston so many years before, was now and precariously Prime Minister. From the House of Lords he adroitly steered the Abolition Bill to victory, and then in the Commons it became clear that the measure was safe. It passed its crucial second reading by 283 to 16 votes. It received the royal assent in the nick of time before Grenville's ministry fell.

The well known epilogue took place probably not in Clapham but in Wilberforce's Westminster house in Palace Yard. "Well, Henry," he said to Thornton, "What shall we abolish next?" William Smith cried out "Let us make out the names of those 16 miscreants". "Never mind the miserable 16," said Wilberforce, "let us think of our glorious 283!"

But of course the trade was not abolished nor could it be stopped by a British Act of Parliament. The English share had been a high proportion of the total traffic but the concurrence of other European powers was necessary, smuggling had to be stopped and the oceans had to be patrolled. Denmark and Holland had already concurred, and as the tide turned against Napoleon during the next years, it was also flowing in favour of abolition.

The conscience of Britain had been permanently awakened, the strength of public opinion encouraged diplomatic efforts to get general European agreement. After Napoleon's defeat at Leipzig and exile to Elba, the Sect mounted a lightning campaign. Within a few weeks 800 petitions poured into the House of Commons, nearly a million signatures made plain the wishes of the public. Leaflets and pamphlets in French and German were spread abroad by the African Institution which had now replaced the Abolition Committee. "No clearer mandate has ever been given by public opinion to a diplomat than that which Castlereagh (the Foreign Secretary) took with him to Vienna"[16] where the Congress was assembled to negotiate the peace treaties.

Thomas Clarkson addresses
the Anti-Slavery Society Convention, 1840.
Benjamin Robert Haydon, 1841.

Paris was the main problem. The Republic had abolished the slave trade, but Napoleon had restored it. Now the French desired to resume their share of the trade. Talleyrand, the slippery French Foreign Minister, eluded all efforts at agreement, though the restored French king, Louis XVIII, was an abolitionist. But there was a somewhat unexpected ally in the Duke of Wellington who, after chasing Napoleon's troops over the Pyrenees, was made ambassador in Paris. After the 'Hundred days' return of Napoleon from Elba and his final defeat at Waterloo (1815) the Iron Duke's hand was greatly strengthened, and he had long decided with military directness that the trade was wrong and must stop. He personally organised the distribution of abolitionist propaganda and persuaded the formidable Madame de Staël to translate its documents. "C'est vous et Lord Wellington" she wrote to Wilberforce, "qui aurez gagné cette grande bataille pour l'humanité".

When Portugal and then Spain were partly persuaded and partly bribed to concur, all countries which had engaged in the trade had given their agreement. The Royal Navy, now comparatively under-employed, took over the task of patrolling the seas, and slaves thus liberated could be given refuge in Sierra Leone.

This, we might claim, was Clapham's finest hour. The work of the Sect had transformed the moral climate of the nation. Wilberforce in a way had become its conscience, and also that of Europe. When the sovereign princes and statesmen of Europe gathered in London to celebrate the peace, one by one they insisted on meeting Wilberforce. The King of Prussia presented him with a set of Dresden china, the Czar consulted him. By the people of England he was greatly beloved, he was besieged by admirers, petitioners and disciples, his correspondence was phenomenal, village bells were set ringing when he was said to be in the neighbourhood.

WILBERFORCE'S CRITICS

HE WAS NOT, HOWEVER, UNIVERSALLY BELOVED. Many sincere and moderate churchmen regarded Evangelicals as fanatics, particularly as they grew in influence and importance. The best of these critics and the best of men was the Reverend Sydney Smith, who eventually became a Canon of St Paul's. His wit and brilliance, his sincere and sensible religion (our Sect would have denied that such a thing is possible) made his onslaught in the *Edinburgh Review* especially effective. "I would counsel my lords the Bishops to keep their eyes on that holy village…"

Other critics, above all writers in Canning's *Anti-Jacobin Review*, used the tactics of the sledge-hammer, accusing Zachary Macaulay (of all people) of feathering his own nest, and the Evangelicals of using the "immense profits which accrue from their trade in philanthropy" to buy boroughs and so increase their power in Parliament to spread "schism over the land", and so on.

The most frequent criticism was that these fanatics were indifferent to the sufferings of their own countrymen as they ranged the earth in order to break the fetters of the slave. Charity begins at home was recommended. This particular line is somewhat easier to defend from contemporaries than it is from critics in our own time, for the numerous domestic charities of the Sect were largely private while their chief public support was dedicated to this world cause.

Wilberforce's bitterest critics were the Radicals. They detested him for his support of those periods of repression both during and after the war which Tory governments considered necessary to prevent revolution; for his support of the Corn Laws passed to help the 'landed interest' after the Peace and which kept up the price of bread, and for his pro-government role in a horrible affair in 1819. A peaceful rally of about 50,000 men and women and children in St Peter's Fields in Manchester to demand Parliamentary reform was hustled by the Yeomanry and charged by sword-wielding Hussars – this was the 'Massacre of Peterloo'. The magistrates responsible were supported by the Government and even more repressive legislation was passed. It is not surprising the Radicals such as William Cobbett hated Wilberforce.

Wilberforce was certainly not progressive in his social policies, he accepted the structures of society of his day, but it is perhaps unjust to call him a reactionary. He insisted on the importance of temporary acts against sedition, he sympathised with the moves to reform the savage penal code and with the campaign against the Game Laws against poaching. But his social philanthropy was directed to alleviating the suffering caused or tolerated by a system he accepted. He never, for example, modified his support for the Combination Laws which forbade the growth of the early trade unions. It is unfortunate that in its new Calendar the Church of England should have assigned a day for remembrance of Wilberforce, as a "social reformer". He was so many other things, but not that.

The Sect took the same pragmatic attitude in politics. During the bleak period after Waterloo, Wilberforce and the Sect were moving to the left of the Tory party, especially on the key issues of Catholic emancipation and parliamentary reform. While the old system lasted they were, however, quite ready to continue to work within it. When Wilberforce became too old and frail to continue as Member of Parliament for Yorkshire, he gladly accepted the cosiest of pocket boroughs "as a gift from a noble relative of his wife," who begged him in the kindest manner possible to consider Bramber, a tiny village in Sussex, "quite as my own".

"Which was worse, British poverty or West Indian slavery?"
Anti-abolition cartoon from
The Looking Glass, 1832.

Abolition of slavery

IT WAS DURING THIS PERIOD that the campaign to abolish slavery was determined on by the men who had abolished the British slave trade. Wilberforce was unable to lead this crusade. "It is suitable for an aged Christian to show himself willing to retire and let others take the more leading stations", he said. He likened himself to Moses and chose as his Joshua the young Quaker, Thomas Fowell Buxton.

By this time, Clapham could no longer claim to be the centre or base of operations. Wilberforce had moved to Westminster in 1808, and thence to Kensington Gore, in 1802 the Grants had moved back to Bloomsbury, followed later by Macaulay, and Stephen had moved to Great Ormond Street. Venn and Granville Sharp died in 1813, and Thornton in 1815. To history however they are ever known as the Clapham Sect and their remarkable achievements can rightly be claimed by the village where they became a fraternity whose shared faith and pooled talents and labours had empowered them to change the world.

When Wilberforce decided to leave Parliament altogether and applied for the Chiltern Hundreds in 1825, Thomas Fowell Buxton quoted the inscription which the Carthaginians carved on the tomb of Hannibal, "We vehemently desired him in the day of battle."

Stephen, Clarkson and Macaulay were still on the field, and the Anti-Slavery Society had taken over the campaign from the African Institution. Macaulay's *Anti-Slavery Monthly* was "compiled and written with painstaking thoroughness and stark realism".[17] Wilberforce continued to support their titanic drudgery and vehement industry. In 1833 he emerged from his retirement to support a meeting at Maidstone: "It shall never be said that William Wilberforce is silent while the slaves require his help." It was his last public appearance.

The climax had arrived. In 1833 Edward Stanley (later Lord Derby), Colonial Secretary in the new Whig government of Lord Grey, introduced in the recently reformed Parliament the Abolition Bill, drafted in his department by young James Stephen – he who was reading in the Oval Library many years before. James, now Under-Secretary in the Colonial Office, drafted the Bill in two days, one of which was a Sunday, the first and only time when he sacrificed his Sabbatarian principles to a task "which had devolved upon me by inheritance." His father had died just a year before.

Wilberforce, who lay dying in his friend William Smith's house in Cadogan Place, rejoiced to hear of the passage of the clause to compensate the slave owners – "That I should have lived to witness a day in which England is willing to give 20 millions sterling for the abolition of slavery". With his death the Clapham Sect must be said to have come to an end.

Viscount Tonypandy, formerly Speaker of the House of Commons, accepting gifts on behalf of Holy Trinity on 29 July 1983: GLC Councillor Paul Boateng (later MP and the first black Cabinet Minister) presents a facsimile of the new Blue Plaque.

The heritage of the Clapham Sect

THE WORK OF THE CLAPHAM SECT WAS NOT DONE however, and they left a heritage which shaped the rest of the century.

Long before the first dose of Parliamentary Reform in 1832 they had helped to reform the moral climate of politics. Claphamites who became MPs were incorruptible and even while operating under the old system they had reduced bribery in elections. Thornton at Southwark had stoutly refused to pay the customary £1 a vote, Wilberforce in Yorkshire had reduced expenditure on bribery. There were 16,000 freehold voters in the huge constituency. In 1807, as an example, he spent £28,000, largely on conveying voters to the poll in York, his opponents spent £200,000. He was returned with a solid majority.

In 1828, Dissenters were enfranchised, and the 1832 Reform Act largely enfranchised the middle classes and gave cities such as Birmingham and Manchester representatives in Parliament. Constitutional, economic and social problems now had to be tackled by a partnership of the old political leadership, still very much in the saddle, and the new electorate.

The Utilitarians, followers of Jeremy Bentham, sometimes called secular Evangelicals, with their "greatest happiness of the greatest number" principle of moral and political arithmetic, were a powerful force, with which the Clapham Sect tradition and experience could well co-operate. William Smith had long worked closely with them.

Probably the most important Clapham Sect contribution to the hesitant beginnings of modern democracy (a word they would not have used) was in the creation, informing and marshalling of public opinion, especially of the middle classes, often non-conformist in allegiance.

The techniques developed by the great Clapham crusades became the method by which responsible and active public life was lived in the new society.

They invented the Public Cause, and the Anniversary: we cannot claim that they invented the committee, but surely they made the committee a way of life. As the younger James Stephen wrote in 1849, "Ours is the age of societies. For the redress of every repression that is done under the sun there is a public meeting, for the cure of every sorrow by which our land or our race can be visited, there are patrons, vice-presidents and secretaries. For the diffusion of every blessing of which mankind can partake in common, there is a committee...". We begin to recognise ourselves.

Clapham provided a frame of mind for the new age, and much of the apparatus by which it operated. It also even more directly supplied its agents. The next generation of Claphamites had remarkable talents which helped to form the intellectual aristocracy which ran the schools, founded the new universities, reformed and staffed the Civil Service, ran the learned societies, published the journals and so forth.

Samuel Wilberforce became Bishop of Oxford, James Stephen the younger Under-Secretary for the Colonies, young Charles Grant, Lord Glenelg, Colonial Secretary in Lord Grey's cabinet, Thomas Macaulay the most renowned historian of the century, Henry Venn became Chief Secretary of the Church Missionary Society from 1841–1872. William Smith's grandchildren included Florence Nightingale and Barbara Leigh-Smith, Madame Bodichon, co-founder of Girton College at Cambridge, the first such college for women. The Bonham-Carter family were also his descendants. James Stephen's wife was John Venn's daughter, his son Leslie was the founder and editor of the *Dictionary of National Biography*, Leslie's daughters were Virginia Woolf, and Vanessa Bell. E M Forster was Henry Thornton's great grandson.

Moreover these Clapham families intermarried with Trevelyans, Arnolds, Fosters, Wedgwoods, Darwins, Huxleys, Wards, Stracheys. Some of these were from a very different quarry, the secular radical tradition of the Utilitarians, the inheritors of the Enlightenment. The 'in-house' poet of these joint traditions, Matthew Arnold, analysed society into barbarians, philistines, and aliens; these were the aliens. They were able to criticise society with detachment, and did not identify themselves with particular interests.

By the end of the century, Bloomsbury had replaced Clapham as a circle which influenced the outlook of a generation. They were literary, aesthetic and intellectual rather than philanthropic, unless a tinge of Fabian Socialism can count as such. They were not good at committees.

Evangelical beliefs had permeated society by the early years of Queen Victoria, but their very success brought the weakness of nominal adherents and in any case they failed to satisfy later generations intellectually and spiritually. The weakness of the Evangelicals was that they neither gave nor required a metaphysical explanation of the riddle of the universe. Gladstone declared that they treated the redemption of man as "a joint-stock enterprise with Christ as the broker".

In the great days of the Clapham Sect these deficiencies were obscured by the stature of the agents and their heroic commitment to titanic causes. The chief battle won, the weaknesses became apparent. Wilberforce had been content to say, "I'm not here to speculate, but to repent". This would not do for their descendants; the divorce of piety and intellect had become unacceptable.

SHAPING WORLD HISTORY

GREAT CLAIMS HAVE BEEN MADE for the Clapham Sect's place in world history. Can they be justified? The most uncompromising denial comes from economic historians, notably Eric Williams (later to become Prime Minister of Trinidad) whose *Capitalism and Slavery* (1944) held that the plantation system and the trade that fed it was inefficient and declining in prosperity and would have disappeared without the exertions of the abolitionists. The Clapham Sect was wasting its time and effort.

This would have been startling news to Wilberforce, Clarkson and their circle, confronted with vehement, violent and unscrupulous 'West Indians' and their supporters, maintaining that the slave trade was essential to their economic survival. Recent research, led especially by the late Professor Anstey of the University of Kent, confirms that the plantation system was actually increasing in profitability. The debate will probably never be satisfactorily settled for it is between two opposing views of history, and precise and conclusive evidence is difficult to find. But in view of the toughness of the surviving institution of slavery and of trade in slaves, Clapham is justified in inclining to the support of the Sect's reputation.

They had carried through just in time the most urgent task. If the African slave trade and imperial slave plantations had lasted until economic, technical and political developments had opened up and colonised the African continent, the results would have been horrible beyond imagination. The social and economic effects on Europe also could not be calculated. The historian G M Trevelyan (himself part of the Clapham family tree) considered that the consequences would have "destroyed and corrupted Europe itself". Bad as the colonial record in Africa has been, the European powers had decided that "slavery should not be the relation of the black man to the white".[18]

IMPERIALISM AND MISSION

THE AGE OF IMPERIALISM WAS UPON THE WORLD. By the mid-nineteenth century exploration had often been followed by exploitation and colonisation. Here the inheritance of the Clapham Sect ensured that missionaries followed, sometimes preceded, the traders, settlers, and administrators. This is not the place to discuss the rightness or wrongness of Christian missions, but it is certain that without the missionaries, even if they sometimes erred into religious and cultural imperialism, the situation would have been much worse. Thomas Macaulay's famous *Minute* (1835) on Indian education was a case in point. As member of the Council in Calcutta he was concerned with the question of the medium of instruction in the schools – English, or the classic languages of India? Macaulay, apparently unimpressed by Indian wisdom, proposed that it should be English, to create an intellectual elite, "thoroughly at home in western languages and sciences," which should then diffuse useful knowledge throughout the population. In fact the elite left the second part of this policy to be carried out by the missionaries. It is difficult to make a moral or an historical judgment on the matter but instructive to try to imagine India not integrated into a world culture based on the English language and European-American thought systems and knowledge.

The same problem arises in Africa. Much of the exploration of the 'dark continent' was the logical continuation of Clapham crusades. Livingstone, pursuing his all-consuming passion to discover the sources of the Nile, laid open the very heart of Africa and revealed the full atrocities of the continuing slave trade. He died far from any white man in 1873 and his last recorded words echoed those of the Sect: "All I can say in my solitude is… may Heaven's rich blessing come down on everyone – American, English, Turk – who will help to heal this open sore of the world".

The missionary societies were steadily penetrating the continent. The west coast was guarded by intrepid squadrons of mosquitoes, but equally intrepid, and often short-lived, missionaries persevered in their task. Sierra Leone failed as a useful base and has had a sorry history to this day, but in 1872 the Church Missionary Society founded there "an incomparable service to the whole of West Africa",[19] Fourah Bay College for the higher education of Africans.

Henry Venn, Chief Secretary of the Church Missionary Society was a consummate administrator and mission strategist. His *Minute* of 1861 defined the aim of missions as to create self-governing and self-supporting churches, "the euthanasia of mission". Early attempts to carry out this policy and to consecrate African bishops were not successful, but in time modifications of the policy were worked out and the attempt was perhaps in itself an achievement.

The position today is strikingly shown by the Lambeth Conference of the Anglican world communion in 1998. At this recent conference world-wide Anglican policy was shaped by the African bishops, unwilling to accept the trends of American and European moral thinking. Probably few of the bishops knew much about the Clapham Sect and the important part which our village played in creating the world in which we live today.

Epilogue

C LAPHAM MUST PROVIDE THE POST-SCRIPT. E M Forster's *Domestic Biography* of his great-aunt Marianne Thornton (1797–1887) recreates the family life of the Sect, and gives a child's eye view of events and people.

Little Marianne recollected the fear of Napoleon; she was convinced that he would come and cut down the tulip tree in the garden of Battersea Rise House, but little Tom Macaulay stoutly reassured her that he would only stab all the children to death in their beds. Once there was a Twelfth Night fancy dress party at Lord Teignmouth's – young Wilberforce went as the Pope. Marianne recalled that "one of many first lessons was I must never disturb Papa when he was talking or reading, but no such prohibition existed with Mr Wilberforce". He was "as restless and volatile as a child himself and always ready to be interrupted, perhaps to have a race on the lawn 'to warm his feet' ". Or the large and loud Dr Milner saying " 'Now Wilberforce listen for no power will make me repeat what I am going to say...' when Mr W (sic) was flitting after a child, a cat, a flower or a new book".

She has idyllic recollections of visits to Cowslip Green in Somerset to stay with Mrs Hannah More and her sister, their friendly and affectionate servants, and the two cats, Non-Resistance and Passive Obedience. The Clapham children certainly had happy childhoods – the style of upbringing could be called Evangelical-Rousseauesque.

In 1815 Henry Thornton died of consumption and his wife did not long survive him. Marianne was eighteen, the youngest of the nine children only five. Congenial guardians came to look after them, and Battersea Rise House and its gardens remained a beloved home, and so it continued until Clapham's last crusade, almost a parody of the great ones of the past.

The eldest son and heir to the bank, Henry Sykes Thornton, having lost his first wife, daughter of the Rector, Dr Dealtry, desired to marry her sister. This was not allowed under existing law, and so began the campaign for the right to marry one's deceased wife's sister. Today such a cause might stir up little passion, but in 1850 it aroused immense moral

Harriet, William and Emily Dealtry
in the garden at Battersea Rise.
inset: Marianne Thornton.

indignation. Henry withdrew to Europe to be married and remained an exile for some time. It was the break up of the family and the home. When Henry and his wife returned to Battersea Rise House they were not 'received by society', nor by the family. Only Marianne, who had moved to a house at 1 The Sweep, on the Pavement, where Trinity Close now stands, quietly kept up some contact with her brother. He died in 1892, long before in 1907 the law was passed which allowed marriage with the deceased wife's sister.

In that same year the Battersea Rise estate was sold and the house demolished, the beautiful gardens and meadows disappeared beneath numerous terraces of houses. A few street names survive to remind us today of this power-house of the Clapham Sect.

Their true power-house, Holy Trinity Church, keeps their memorials and their memory. It is right that Clapham should remember that "The unweary, unostentatious and unglorious crusade of England against slavery may probably be regarded as among the three or four perfectly virtuous pages comprised in the history of nations."[20]

REFERENCES

(1) David Cecil, *The Stricken Deer*, is an account of their friendship
(2) E Halévy, *History of the English People in 1815*, (1924), p383
(3) James Stephen, *Essays in Ecclesiastical Biography*, (1849), p206
(4) Reginald Coupland, *Wilberforce*, p77
(5) Ignatius Latrobe in 1815 – Coupland, pp78-9
(6) Gillian Clegg, *Clapham*, p44, ascribes this to Boswell
(7) Ford K Brown, *Fathers of the Victorians*
(8) Stephen, p190
(9) Stephen, p224-5
(10) J W Ashley Smith, *The Birth of Modern Education*

(11) Coupland, quoted by Howse, p71
(12) Millennium lecture to the Historical Association
(13) Michael Hennell, *John Venn and the Clapham Sect*, p284
(14) John Owen, historian of the Bible Society, in 1816
(15) Coupland, p247
(16) Coupland, p329
(17) E M Howse, *Saints in Politics*, p162
(18) Howse, p178
(19) Stephen Neill, *A History of Christian Missions*, p306
(20) W E H Lecky, *History of European Morals*, (1877), I p153

Biographical notes

A brief biographical index to the main people mentioned in this booklet.

BABINGTON, THOMAS (1758–1837). MP, Leicestershire landowner and brother-in-law of Zachary Macaulay.
BUXTON, THOMAS FOWELL (1786–1845). MP, brewer, prison reformer and a Quaker. Succeeded Wilberforce as leading Parliamentary campaigner against slavery.
CLARKSON, THOMAS (1760–1846). Campaigner against the slave trade and slavery.
ELIOT, EDWARD (1759–97). MP, brother-in-law of William Pitt.
ELLIOTT, CHARLES (1751–1832). Wealthy London merchant. Brother-in-law of John Venn.
FOX, CHARLES JAMES (1749–1806). MP, leading Whig opponent of Pitt. Foreign Secretary in Grenville ministry, 1806.
GISBORNE, THOMAS (1758–1846). Staffordshire clergyman. Friend of Wilberforce.
GRANT, CHARLES (1746–1823). MP. Director of the East India Company. Promoter of missionary and educational work in India.
GRENVILLE, WILLIAM, Baron Grenville (1759–1834). Minister in Pitt's government. Prime Minister 1806–7.
MACAULAY, ZACHARY (1768–1838). Governor of Sierra Leone. Editor of the *Christian Observer*. Father of the historian THOMAS MACAULAY (Lord Macaulay) (1800–59).
MANSFIELD, LORD (1705–93). Lord Chief Justice 1756–88. Gave many important judgments in contentious cases, including that of the runaway slave, James Somersett.

MILNER, ISAAC (1750–1820). Clergyman, theologian and mathematician. President of Queens' College, Cambridge and Dean of Carlisle.
MORE, HANNAH (1745–1833). Educationalist and popular writer of religious and moral works.
NEWTON, JOHN (1725–1807). Former slave trader, became clergyman. Curate of Olney, Bucks, then Rector of St Mary Woolnoth in the City of London.
PITT, WILLIAM the younger (1759–1806). Son of Prime Minister William Pitt, Earl of Chatham. MP, and Prime Minister aged 24. Friend of Wilberforce and opposed to the slave trade, but rendered cautious by the French Revolution and the opposition to abolition of King George III.
SHARP, GRANVILLE (1735–1813). Self-taught lawyer, fought cases to establish that slavery could not be enforced in England.
SHORE, JOHN, Lord Teignmouth (1751–1834). Governor General of India.
SIMEON, CHARLES (1759–1836). Clergyman and fellow of King's College Cambridge. Leading Evangelical.
SMITH, SYDNEY (1771–1845). Clergyman and wit. Canon of St Paul's.
SMITH, WILLIAM (1756–1835). MP, supporter of Charles James Fox.
STEPHEN, JAMES (1758–1832). Lawyer and MP. Brother-in-law of Wilberforce. His son SIR JAMES STEPHEN (1789–1859), a civil servant, prepared the bill abolishing slavery in 1833.
THORNTON, HENRY (1760–1815). MP, banker and economist. Youngest son of John Thornton. Abolitionist and supporter of missionary activities. Father of Marianne Thornton.
THORNTON, JOHN (1720–90). Wealthy merchant and banker. Financial supporter of evangelical clergy. Father of SAMUEL THORNTON (1754–1838), MP and Bank of England Director, and of Robert and Henry.
VENN, HENRY (1725–97). Clergyman. Curate of Clapham, Vicar of Huddersfield, Rector of Yelling (Huntingdonshire).
VENN, JOHN (1759–1813). Clergyman, son of Henry Venn. Rector of Clapham 1792–1813. Father of Henry Venn, Secretary of the CMS.
WILBERFORCE, WILLIAM (1759–1833). MP. Parliamentary leader of the campaign against the slave trade. Active supporter of other humanitarian and religious causes. Author of influential '*Practical view...*'. Father of Bishop Samuel Wilberforce.

Reading

THE NEAREST CONTEMPORARY ACCOUNT is *Studies in Ecclesiastical Biography* (Longman, 1849), reprints of articles in the *Edinburgh Review* of 1838 and 1843 by Sir James Stephen.

A general account is Ernest Marshall Howse, *Saints in Politics, the "Clapham Sect" and the Growth of Freedom* (Allen & Unwin, 1953). This has been set as an Open University text. Ford K Brown, *Fathers of the Victorians, the Age of Wilberforce* (OUP, 1962) is a massive, unsympathetic work, over-loaded with (useful) quotations. More recent, comprehensive and judicious is Professor Roger Anstey, *The Atlantic Slave Trade & British Abolition, 1760–1801* (Cambridge Commonwealth Series, Macmillan, 1975). *Anti-Slavery Religion & Reform* (Dawson & Archer, 1980) contains essays in memory of Professor Anstey, edited by C Bolt and S Drescher. This gives a European perspective.

The biography of *Wilberforce* (Collins, 1945) by Reginald Coupland, who was Professor of Colonial History at Oxford, is a splendid and perceptive read. *Granville Sharp* by Edward Lascelles (OUP, 1928) and *Hannah More* by M G Jones (CUP, 1952) are delightful and illuminating. Michael Hennell *John Venn & the Clapham Sect* (Lutterworth, 1958) is very useful, especially for the local aspect. R W Davis, *Dissent in Politics, the Political Life of William Smith MP* (Epworth Press, 1971) is thorough and scholarly. George Otto Trevelyan, *The Life and Letters of Lord Macaulay* (1876) gives material about Zachary Macaulay and the family, and Noel Annan, *Leslie Stephen* (Macgibbon & Kee, 1951) does so for the Stephen family. It also introduces Dr Annan's specialty, the family ramifications of the "Intellectual

Aristocracy of Victorian England". This is more fully developed in *Studies in Social History*, essays in honour of G M Trevelyan, edited by J H Plumb (Longman, 1955).

The Dictionary of National Biography has biographies of the leaders of the Clapham Sect and other political figures. *The Dictionary of Evangelical Biography*, ed. D M Lewis (Blackwell, 1995) covers a very wide range of clergy and lay people active in the religious revival. A specialist background work is Stephen Neill, *A History of Christian Missions, the Pelican History of the Church 6* (Penguin, 1964).

Spanish Town, Jamaica.
Procession celebrating the abolition
of slavery, 1838.

INDEX

Abolition Committee 16-18, 22, 46
African Institution 46, 50
American War of Independence 7, 14, 30
Anti-Slavery Monthly 50
Australia 35
Babington, Thomas 9, 13, 30, 37-38, 41
Battersea Rise House 26-27, 29, 33-34, 57-59
Bible Society, The 41-42
Brookes, slave ship 19
Broomwood House 26, 29
Buxton, Thomas Fowell 11, 50

Cambridge 10, 17-18, 21, 37
Christian Observer, The 40-41
Church Missionary Society 36-38, 42, 53, 56
Clapham Armed Association 24
Clapham Poor Society 24
Clarkson, Thomas 9, 11, 16-19, 30, 32, 44, 46, 50, 54
Cowper, William 10

Dealtry, Dr William 41, 58

East India Company 27, 35, 36, 38
Eclectic Society 37, 41
Eliot, Edward 9, 26
Elliott, Charles 9, 13, 26, 37, 41

Forster, EM 25, 53, 57
Fox, Charles James 12, 21, 31, 44-45
French Revolution 18, 24, 43-44

Gisborne, Thomas 9, 13, 41
Glenelg 27, 29

Grant, Charles 9, 27-30, 32, 35-38, 41, 43, 50
Grenville, William, Lord 45

Hatchard, John 41
Holy Trinity Church 8-9, 13, 22-23, 26, 29, 32, 37-38, 51, 59
Huddersfield 10
Hull 18, 21, 23

India 27-28, 35-38, 42-43, 55-56

Jamaica 14, 28, 63

Keston, Vale of 18, 45

Macaulay, Thomas, Lord 31, 53, 55, 57
Macaulay, Zachary 9, 11, 13, 28-32, 37, 41, 48, 50
Mansfield, Lord 14-15, 30
Middleton, Sir Charles and Lady 17-18
Milner, Isaac 10, 21, 57
More, Hannah 10, 13, 18-19, 31, 39-41, 57

Napoleon 7, 24, 31, 44-47, 57
Newton, John 10, 18, 21
North Side, Clapham Common 26, 31

Old Town 26
Orangery 24

Peterloo Massacre 48
Pitt, William, the younger 9, 18, 21, 26, 33, 35, 43-45

Ramsay, James 16
Rectory Grove 31
Religious Tract Society 39, 41
Richmond, Legh 40
Sharp, Granville 9, 11, 14-18, 29-32, 41, 50

Sheridan, Richard Brinsley 12
Shore, John (Lord Teignmouth) 9, 27-29, 32, 37, 42, 57
Sierra Leone 30-31, 42, 47, 56
Simeon, Charles 10
Smith, Sydney 10, 22, 47
Smith, William 9, 29, 32-34, 39, 45, 51-53
Somersett, James 15
South Side, Clapham Common 23, 33
Stephen, James, the elder 9, 12-13, 28-29, 32, 37-38, 41, 43-45, 50
Stephen, James, the younger 13, 33, 51, 53
Strong, Jonathan 14

Teignmouth *see* Shore
Teston 16, 18
Thornton, Henry 9, 13, 21, 24-26, 29-30, 32, 35-39, 41, 43, 45, 50, 52, 53, 57, 59
Thornton, John 23, 24-25, 29, 32
Thornton, Marianne 25, 57-59
Thornton, Samuel 24, 25, 27, 42

Venn, Henry 8, 10, 23, 29, 32
Venn, Henry, the younger 53, 56
Venn, John 9, 13, 23-24, 26, 27, 29, 32, 36-37, 39-40, 50

Wellington, Duke of 47
Wesley, John 10, 12, 15, 40
Wilberforce, William 9-13, 18, 20-23, 25-30, 32-41, 43-45, 47-52, 54, 57

[64]